PETS UP CLOSE

Pebble® Plus

Pet Hermit Crabs

UP CLOSE

by Jeni Wittrock

Gail Saunders-Smith, PhD, Consulting Editor

CAPSTONE PRESS
a capstone imprint

Pebble Plus is published by Capstone Press,
1710 Roe Crest Drive, North Mankato, Minnesota 56003
www.capstonepub.com

Library of Congress Cataloging-in-Publication Data
Wittrock, Jeni, author.
Pet Hermit Crabs Up Close / by Jeni Wittrock.
pages cm.—(Pebble Plus. Pets Up Close)
Summary: "Full-color, zoomed-in photos and simple text describe pet hermit crabs' body parts"—Provided by publisher.
Audience: Ages 5-8.
Audience: K to grade 3.
Includes bibliographical references and index.
ISBN 978-1-4914-2109-3 (library binding)
ISBN 978-1-4914-2323-3 (paperback)
ISBN 978-1-4914-2350-9 (eBook PDF)
1. Hermit crabs as pets—Juvenile literature.
2. Hermit crabs—Anatomy—Juvenile .literature. I. Title.
SF459.H47W58 2015
639.67—dc23   2014036383

Editorial Credits
Bobbie Nuytten, designer; Gina Kammer, media researcher; Gene Bentdahl, production specialist

Photo Credits
All photographs by Capstone Studio: Karon Dubke

The author thanks her patient, tolerant, and outgoing pet hermit crabs, who are seen in the photos in this book. When she's in a pinch for great photos, the hermies always come through!

Note to Parents and Teachers

The Pets Up Close set supports national science standards related to life science. This book describes and illustrates pet hermit crabs. The images support early readers in understanding the text. The repetition of words and phrases helps early readers learn new words. This book also introduces early readers to subject-specific vocabulary words, which are defined in the Glossary section. Early readers may need assistance to read some words and to use the Table of Contents, Glossary, Read More, Internet Sites, and Index sections of the book.

Printed in the United States of America in Stevens Point, Wisconsin.
092014   008479WZS15

Table of Contents

At Home on the Go

Which pet carries its home
wherever it goes?
A hermit crab!
Let's learn all about these
shell-wearing animals!

Walking Legs

Four walking legs help hermit crabs walk, dig, and climb. Their legs have hairy setae to feel what's nearby.

say setae like this: SEE-tay

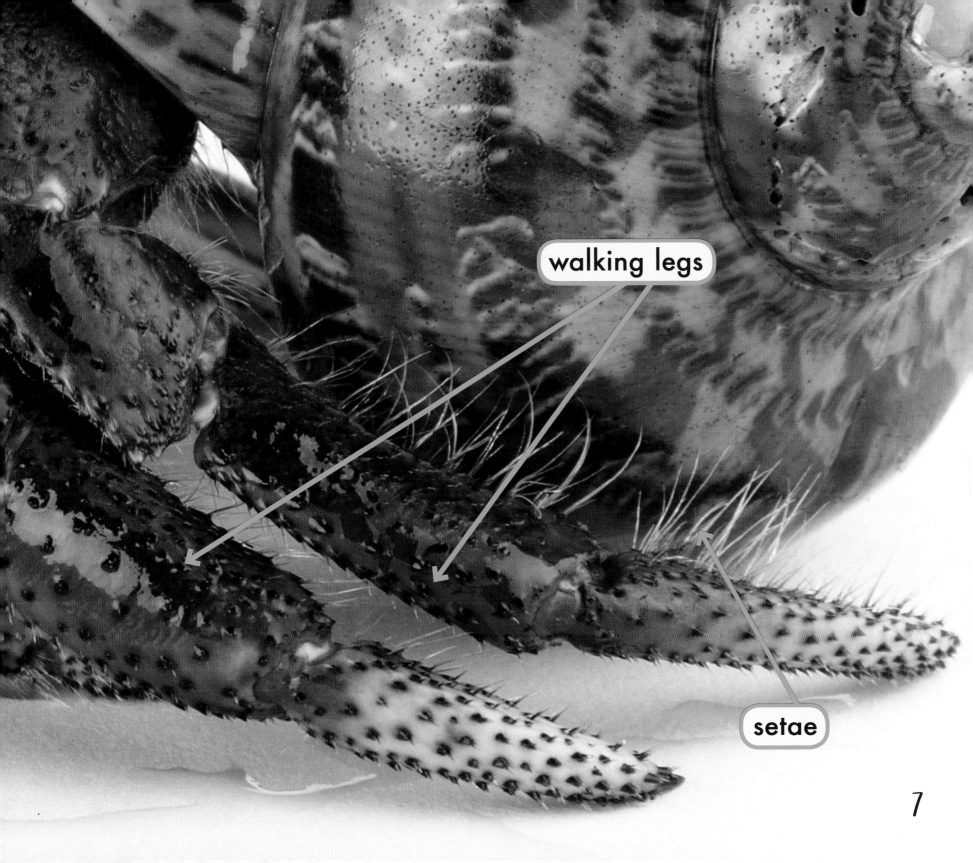

walking legs

setae

7

Eyes

Hermit crabs' eyes sit on top of eyestalks. Tall eyes are perfect for spotting movement. Good sight helps hermies stay away from predators.

eye

eyestalk

9

Carapace

A hermit crab's back has
a hard cover or carapace.
The carapace protects
a crab's soft insides.

carapace

11

Pincers

A hermit crab's front legs
have claws called pincers.
Big claws pick up food
and hold things tightly.

13

Gills

Hermit crabs come from near the ocean. They breathe through slits called gills. Gills are perfect for breathing warm, wet ocean air.

gills

Antennas

Look at those wiggly antennas!
Two straight antennae help
feel the way when it's dark.
Two bent antennas smell
and taste food.

Mouthparts

Dinnertime! Hermit crabs have six little mouthparts. A hermit's claws lift food up to its mouthparts. Then mouthparts move the food to its mouth.

mouthparts

No Place Like Home

Hermit crabs don't stay in one shell too long. As they grow, hermits move into bigger shells. Safe inside their shells, busy hermies can rest. Zzz...

Glossary

antennae—feelers on a hermit crab's head used to touch, taste, and smell; antennae is the word for more that one antenna

carapace—the hard part on a hermit crab's back

eyestalk—the part that holds up the eye of a hermit crab

gill—one of many slits that are used for breathing

mouthpart—a tiny bodypart that lifts food to a hermit crab's mouth

pincer—a claw used to grab and pinch

predator—an animal that hunts other animals for food

seta—one of many hairs, or setae, that feel movement and vibrations

Read More

Binns, Tristan Boyer. *Hermit Crabs.* Keeping Unusual Pets. Chicago: Heinemann Library, 2010.

Carraway, Rose. *Happy Hermit Crabs.* Pet Corner. New York: Gareth Stevens Pub., 2012.

Silverstein, Alvin. *Hermit Crabs: Cool Pets!* Far-Out and Unusual Pets. Berkeley Heights, N.J.: Enslow Elementary, 2011.

Internet Sites

FactHound offers a safe, fun way to find Internet sites related to this book. All of the sites on FactHound have been researched by our staff.

Here's all you do:

Visit *www.facthound.com*

Type in this code: 9781491421093

Check out projects, games and lots more at **www.capstonekids.com**

Index

Word Count: 189
Grade: 1
Early-Intervention Level: 19